THE IMPOSSIBILITY OF NOW

a comedy of forgetting and remembering

Y York

BROADWAY PLAY PUBLISHING INC
New York
www.broadwayplaypublishing.com
info@broadwayplaypublishing.com

THE IMPOSSIBILITY OF NOW
© Copyright 2018 Y York

Cover art by Leslie Law

First edition: August 2018
I S B N: 978-0-88145-787-2

Book design: Marie Donovan
Page make-up: Adobe InDesign
Typeface: Palatino

THE IMPOSSIBILITY OF NOW was first produced by Thalia's Umbrella, Seattle, in March 2018. The cast and creative contributors were:

ANTHONY	Joshua Carter
CARL	Terry Edward Moore
MIRANDA	Betsy Schwartz
Director	Daniel Wilson
Stage manager	Jeremiah Givers
Assistant S M	Tallis Moore
Set & lights	Roberta Russell
Sound design	Lucy Peckman
Costume & properties	Kelsey Rogers
Production management	Katie McKellar
Technical direction	Justin Duffiance
Master electrician	Quinn Lincoln
Electrician	Ryan Long

Additional incidental music co-composition
Mark Lutwak, Michael Sakarias, & Lucy Peckman

Graphics design	Leslie Law
Casting	Cornelia Duryèe Moore

THE IMPOSSIBILITY OF NOW was subsequently produced at The Tipping Point Theatre in Northville, Michigan, James R Kuhl, Producing Artistic Director.

CHARACTERS & SETTING

CARL, *male, middle-aged, optimistic, funny, holds off dark clouds. A former science writer.*

MIRANDA, *female, middle-aged, ironic, seeks the sunlight. A poet.*

ANTHONY, *male, middle-aged but younger than the others, attractive, pushy, witty, content to turn on the fluorescents. A dentist.*

Places: Las Vegas. The first floor of a three-story house; a dentist's chair and surroundings; a table at a coffee shop. It's all fluid. No blackouts, except possibly at the end of acts.

Note: There are a lot of words in quotation marks. They are never accompanied by a quotation-mark gesture.

Notes: "…" is a slight hesitation or a shift in tone or intension. "—" is an interruption by the next speaker or the current speaker interrupting him- or herself.

ACT ONE

Scene One

(Tuesday, late in the day. CARL *and* MIRANDA *come into the house. They have a plastic hospital bag, a small suitcase.)*

CARL: There's like a...an array—is that a word?

MIRANDA: Yes. Range, variety—

CARL: There's an array of equipment- tools! camping, or rock climbing, spread out on a blanket? or a...mat!?

MIRANDA: *(Realizing)* I know what that's from—it's a photograph of tools spread out on a large piece of canvas.

CARL: I see the "canvas" on the "ground" full of tools—picks and shovels, but then *(Confused)* I see space, blackness— *(Suddenly)* "space—the final frontier" — what's that mean?

MIRANDA: That's the opening of an old T V show.

CARL: I see space and stars. Am I an astronaut?

MIRANDA: Well. You watched the T V show and that was about astronauts. And you wrote an autobiography for an astronaut.

CARL: *I* wrote it?

MIRANDA: Yes.

CARL: Is that the right word? *Auto* biography?

MIRANDA: You *ghost* wrote it, you remained un-credited.

CARL: Did I mind?

MIRANDA: They paid you a lot.

CARL: How much?

MIRANDA: Two hundred and fifty.

CARL: Is that a lot?

MIRANDA: Thousand. It's a lot.

CARL: The *array*—the "picks" and "shovels" on the "canvas" on the "ground"?— Are they for space?

MIRANDA: No. It's a photo for a different book. One about a dig.

CARL: A Dig?

MIRANDA: Archeology. The study of ancient civilizations. *(Explaining)* Civilizations get buried over time. The archeologist has to...*dig* them up.

CARL: Did they pay me a lot for that book?

MIRANDA: They pay you a lot for everything.

CARL: *(Smiling)* I'm good?

MIRANDA: You're very good.

CARL: *(Happy)* I'm good. Do we spend a lot?

MIRANDA: No. I am not extravagant. We own the house. No mortgage.

CARL: *(Quietly, tasting the word as he looks around.)* "Mortgage." This is mine?

MIRANDA: Ours. Go ahead and look around. He said objects might ignite something.

CARL: *(Enjoying the word)* "Ignite." *(Looking around)* ... Do I *like* it?

MIRANDA: *(Surprised)* Don't you like it?

CARL: Not yet. *Did* I like it?

MIRANDA: It was your idea to buy it. You said renting is lunacy. Financial lunacy.

CARL: Money again. I saw you doing something at the "cashier".

MIRANDA: They wouldn't release you unless I paid. I think we get it all back from the insurance. You should call them.

CARL: *I* should?

MIRANDA: You…you do all that.

CARL: *(Happy)* Okay. *(He is looking around.)*

MIRANDA: *(Referencing the room)* What do you think?

CARL: When they said I could go home, I didn't picture this.

MIRANDA: What did you picture?

CARL: A…an "apartment". Tiny. Four flights of steps.

MIRANDA: That was my cubby hole in Brooklyn.

CARL: *(Savoring the phrase)* "Cubby hole."

MIRANDA: Your apartment was a lot nicer. The one in Pittsburgh.

CARL: How was it nicer?

MIRANDA: It had an elevator, for starters. Three bedrooms. Twelve-foot ceilings. Lots of light. Intricate old woodwork. Our loft is nicer, too. The one in Manhattan. We still own it.

CARL: I pictured four flights of steps. Tiny.

MIRANDA: That was the crummiest place we lived.

CARL: I like it. In my mind I like it.

MIRANDA: Is anything familiar?

CARL: No. Why did I want to live here?

MIRANDA: *(Rattled)* I don't know. You said you liked it. I certainly didn't.

CARL: You don't like it, either?

MIRANDA: It's three stories.

CARL: "Stories." Once upon a time-?

MIRANDA: Three *floors*. Three…flights of steps. Anytime I want something it's on another floor. It's huge and hot and it gets dirty.

CARL: Who cleans it?

MIRANDA: I do.

CARL: I don't help?

MIRANDA: You talk about helping. You mean to help.

CARL: *(Happy, he loves this word)* I'm a shit?

MIRANDA: You get distracted. You stay in your office. We both spend a lot of time on this floor. It's cooler. The heat accumulates upstairs.

CARL: Where's my office?

MIRANDA: In there.

(CARL goes to look at his office. MIRANDA has a moment of tension release. She is at the end of her tether, a deep breath. He re-enters.)

CARL: *(Slightly unsettled)* I don't like it.

MIRANDA: You spend a lot of time in it.

CARL: Why? It's awful.

MIRANDA: *(Rattled)* I don't know—I thought you liked it. …You don't have to stay in there. You can stay in your room, or you can stay in here. You don't have to be in your office.

CARL: No window. All those shelves. It's so dark.

MIRANDA: So you can focus on your work.

CARL: It feels...ominous in there.

MIRANDA: I always thought so.

CARL: We should move.

MIRANDA: No, we shouldn't.

CARL: But if neither one of us likes it-?

MIRANDA: Moving would be hard, and expensive.

CARL: Money. Why does money make me feel funny?

MIRANDA: I don't—I don't even know what you mean. You shouldn't worry.

CARL: *(Joking)* Now that makes me worry.

MIRANDA: *(Exasperated)* Well then, I don't know what to say if I say "don't worry" and that makes you worry, what am I supposed to say?

CARL: I didn't mean to upset you.

MIRANDA: I'm not upset.

CARL: What are you then?

MIRANDA: Its just—all these questions.

CARL: I don't know anything—

MIRANDA: I know— It's just—

CARL: *(Happy, this might be right)* Too much truth.

MIRANDA: Now—*that*. Why did you say *that*? That sounds like you know something.

CARL: I only know what you tell me—

MIRANDA: I've been telling you things for a month— you should...can't you— ...never mind.

(Brief pause)

CARL: *(Joking)* Maybe it's safer to talk about money.

(CARL and MIRANDA both small laugh.)

CARL: How's our money feeling these days?

MIRANDA: Our money is expecting company. There's a settlement.

CARL: "Settlement."

MIRANDA: From the accident.

CARL: I wish I could remember, but there's nothing there. Nothing until I woke up in the hospital and saw you. *(With awe)* Miranda.

MIRANDA: …You remembered the tools- on the ground, on the canvas. Maybe that's how you'll remember- from the things you wrote. You should look at the astronaut book. *(Heading to his office)* It's the most recent. You have photographs of space.

CARL: "Space." *(He inhales suddenly.)*

MIRANDA: *(Returning)* What? What is it?

CARL: "…I was weightless. I pushed myself from one side of the spaceship to the other. My food floated. I squeezed it out of tubes into my mouth. But digestion didn't work right because there was no gravity. We all got cramps. And our bones are hollow because of no gravity. They don't like us to tell the bad stuff. It's all just happy astronauts floating in their spacesuits. They don't want us to talk about waking up in a panic with nowhere to go, trapped and you will stay trapped until you get home, or you die stuck in your orbit with no hope for a rescue with people who you don't know, and you don't like. Robot people. Maybe the others think *I'm* a robot, too."

(CARL and MIRANDA are both amazed.)

CARL: Is that from the book?

MIRANDA: No. It's from your notes. Word-for-word. Word-for-word means—

CARL: I can tell what it means. How long was I in space?

MIRANDA: You weren't in space, Carl. John Hartwell described it to you. The astronaut.

CARL: It feels like a memory, although…incomplete.

MIRANDA: It's John's memory. From your notes.

CARL: Did you read the book?

MIRANDA: I read everything you write. I edit the drafts before your editor gets them.

CARL: So he thinks I'm smarter?

MIRANDA: She. Yes.

CARL: Thank you.

MIRANDA: You do the same for me.

CARL: *(Surprised)* You're a writer, too?

MIRANDA: Both of us.

CARL: I didn't know that.

MIRANDA: *(Some edge)* You didn't ask.

CARL: I didn't?

MIRANDA: No.

CARL: I am so involved with myselfÉ "self-involved" —look at me, right now, I discover a phrase and I forget we're talking about *you*—I am "self-involved".

MIRANDA: Yes, you are.

CARL: I should ask you something.

(Brief pause)

MIRANDA: Well, go ahead!

CARL: Um. What do you write?

MIRANDA: I'm a poet.

CARL: *I* know how to edit a poem?

MIRANDA: *(To herself, but aloud)* You again.

CARL: What?

MIRANDA: Nothing. You *don't* know how to edit a poem. You tell me when I write doggerel.

CARL: *(Loves this word)* "Doggerel." Say a poem.

MIRANDA: I'll give you one to read.

CARL: You don't like to say them?

MIRANDA: I never recite poetry.

CARL: *(For the sake of the word, but it sounds like a command)* "Recite."

MIRANDA: No, I sound phony.

(CARL laughs.)

MIRANDA: No, it's awful. This pretentious voice comes out. It's like a law—when you recite poetry you have to sound phony.

CARL: I know what a poem is.

MIRANDA: Good.

CARL: Yes, it is. I don't know what chromodynamics is. Where did that come from?

MIRANDA: *(Annoyed as it's about him again)* Quarks have colors.

CARL: "Quarks."

MIRANDA: They're tiny, and apparently, colorful. You were helping a physicist write an article. He couldn't explain for shit.

CARL: *(Happy)* It's all for shit. *(Looks around)* My room? You said I can stay in my room? Do I have my own room?

MIRANDA: I…I made up the guestroom.

CARL: We're married.

MIRANDA: You don't even know who I am.

CARL: But you know who I am.

MIRANDA: We should wait.

CARL: How long?

MIRANDA: We should wait until you remember.

CARL: I am deeply missing you.

MIRANDA: As far as you know, you just met me a month ago.

CARL: *(Searches for the word)* The missing feels…feels… *(Brief pause, he looks up, calm but amazed, points)*

MIRANDA: What—what are you looking at?

CARL: Words. They're falling on me like snowflakes. *(Points at a word)* Snow. *(Points at a word)* Flakes. *(Points at a word and follows it down to eye level with his finger:)* Miranda.

(CARL smiles at MIRANDA. Rattled, she exits. He exits.)

Scene Two

(Wednesday afternoon. MIRANDA and ANTHONY in a dental examining room. They are aware of people in the waiting room.)

ANTHONY: *(Disappointed)* Shit. I thought he died.

MIRANDA: Why would you think that?

ANTHONY: You don't come here during office hours.

MIRANDA: Am I not allowed?

ANTHONY: Of course you're allowed—but I thought it was an emergency.

MIRANDA: It is an emergency. One more poem about masculine audacity and I will have to kill one of my students.

ANTHONY: No masculine audacity here. Whatever it is.

MIRANDA: It's growling-and-chest-thumping with rhymes: thumping, bumping, humping…strumpeting. *(Re: waiting room)* What did you tell her?

ANTHONY: You're a very nervous parent who wants to be sure I'm gentle before you bring in your kid.

MIRANDA: That is so sweet. Do parents actually do that?

ANTHONY: No.

MIRANDA: You're a dentist. It still takes me by surprise.

ANTHONY: I'm too buff?

MIRANDA: You're too guy.

ANTHONY: It was my mother's idea when I couldn't turn pro.

MIRANDA: When I first noticed you at the coffee shop I thought you were a casino thug.

ANTHONY: *(Pleased)* A casino thug, really?

MIRANDA: Stop smiling. It's not a compliment.

ANTHONY: No, I know. I have to be careful when I first meet the little patients, so they're not scared.

MIRANDA: They needn't be scared. You are sufficiently gentle.

ANTHONY: *(Sexy)* But not *too* gentle.

MIRANDA: *(Smiles)* Oh, dear. Now I am thinking about how exactly not too gentle you are. I'm thinking about being pleasured in a dental chair.

ANTHONY: *(Glances to the door)* We'll have to be really quiet.

MIRANDA: Anthony, I'm just talking.

ANTHONY: Talking dirty.

MIRANDA: You have an office full of little children.

ANTHONY: And they'll be so sorry when the dentist is late.

MIRANDA: I can't be late to class.

ANTHONY: Quit your job. You can leave your miserable students and your miserable husband at the same time. Come live with me.

MIRANDA: You don't leave a guy in a coma.

ANTHONY: No. You leave a guy out of a coma. You leave a guy faking amnesia to hang onto his wife- who he absolutely does not deserve.

MIRANDA: No one could fake this. I don't even recognize him. Where is the dead-eyed long-distance stare of the last four years? He's so happy. He was never this happy.

ANTHONY: He's trying to make you forget that he's a shit. "Silent, withholding, *indifferent?*" The indifferent Carl- his suck-egg-dog *indifference* to all things Miranda—

MIRANDA: I hate his indifference.

ANTHONY: Who needs the indifference of the dead-eyed Carl when you could be with a guy who wows you with love, care, and…what's the opposite of indifferent?

MIRANDA: Enthusiastic.

ANTHONY: I am the epitome of enthusiastic for all things Miranda.

MIRANDA: He is completely self-involved.

ANTHONY: Just like before. Nothing's changed. He's a shit.

MIRANDA: *(Amazed by this)* He is so happy. Everything is new and…joyous. Don't you wish you could be like that? Everything new?

ANTHONY: *(Beginning to worry)* I do not.

MIRANDA: Every time the first time.

ANTHONY: What's the first time?

MIRANDA: Everything. Words. Sensations.

ANTHONY: Sex?

MIRANDA: I suppose so.

ANTHONY: Oh my God.

MIRANDA: What?

ANTHONY: No—I forgive you.

MIRANDA: Forgive me what—? Oh, for Pete's sake—

ANTHONY: No, I trust you—

MIRANDA: He sleeps in the guestroom- the same place he's been sleeping for the past year. Why would you think that?

ANTHONY: Don't let the new, temporarily-happy Carl erase the miserable soul-sucking silence of the last four years. Four years of your life. Four miserable unhappy years. Until I rescued you. Me. Your hero. We are supposed to be together—I left my wife—

MIRANDA: You did not leave your wife for me.

ANTHONY: Who did I leave her for?

MIRANDA: You were leaving anyway- you did not leave her for me. Don't say that. I am not a home wrecker.

ANTHONY: That's the point. Neither one of us had a home to wreck.

MIRANDA: *(Gestures toward the receptionist)* Shhh.

ANTHONY: *(Lowered voice, a litany)* He's out of the coma, out of the hospital, he has full function, he's home, he's fine. And I am all alone in my brand-new condo-

"completely neutral, nobody's baggage" —a place for us to be together—

MIRANDA: And we will be. Carl will recover, I will leave him, and we will be together. In the meantime, you can get over the bad memory of your marriage.

ANTHONY: I am over my marriage. So over.

MIRANDA: *(Somewhat amused)* You said her name.

ANTHONY: What? I can't say her name?

MIRANDA: You...cried it out.

ANTHONY: I did not. I never did that. ...When?

MIRANDA: Right here in this chair. I wasn't going to mention it— Your residual little longings for Angie.

ANTHONY: Oh yeah, I particularly miss her buying a new Beemer every six months.

MIRANDA: You weren't thinking about a car. More likely her long legs sticking out from under her tiny skirt.

ANTHONY: She dresses like she's fourteen.

MIRANDA: She practically is.

ANTHONY: She is thirty-seven. She just looks...

MIRANDA: What?

ANTHONY: Younger. She looks a little younger.

MIRANDA: I'm not getting a facelift for you.

ANTHONY: No, I love your wrinkles—I said her name because...we're here, in the office—it still reeks of her little visits to show me some expensive useless new item. You should come to the condo.

MIRANDA: She goes there, too.

ANTHONY: To pick up her check- I hand it to her in the hallway so she doesn't sully my surroundings. Please come over. You hate your house.

MIRANDA: So does Carl.

ANTHONY: No. Carl's "fortress". *He* loves it. *You* take care of it.

MIRANDA: He says he hates it. Why did he make us buy if he hates it?

ANTHONY: He's mean and spiteful.

MIRANDA: He is. Why else would he move me to the desert?

ANTHONY: I like the desert—

MIRANDA: Did you see the brown cloud out there?

ANTHONY: I don't go out until I have to.

MIRANDA: It was all his idea. The move. My job? I didn't even know he'd sent them my resume, all of a sudden, we're moving to Las Vegas and I have a teaching job.

ANTHONY: Your husband is a manipulative shit. What does the doctor say?

MIRANDA: About what?

ANTHONY: About when he can be on his own- about his brain!

MIRANDA: Shhh. Carl's brain has un-compartmentalized. Things he's read, written, experienced, all floating around waiting to be remembered, but he can't tell if a memory is from his life or a book he wrote about somebody else.

ANTHONY: Faking.

MIRANDA: No... *(Gets up)* I have class.

ANTHONY: Can you come back after?

MIRANDA: I have to go home after.

ANTHONY: Tomorrow?

MIRANDA: I can't. I'll come after class on Friday.

ANTHONY: That's two whole days.

MIRANDA: One day. One tiny little day.

ANTHONY: *(On his fingers)* Wednesday to Thursday, Thursday to Friday. Two. Two days.

MIRANDA: Wednesday doesn't count because it's today. Friday doesn't count because you'll see me. The only day that counts is Thursday. One tiny little day.

ANTHONY: Don't leave. You have forty-seven minutes.

MIRANDA: Just enough time to get to class.

ANTHONY: I got you something. *(Retrieves a small box from his pocket)*

MIRANDA: No!

ANTHONY: What "no"? I can get you a present.

MIRANDA: I don't have anything for you.

ANTHONY: You gave me your book. Open it.

MIRANDA: It's pretty. What does it do?

ANTHONY: It's a pin. A pen pin. Because you're a poet.

MIRANDA: Did you read the poems?

ANTHONY: Yeah, they're great.

MIRANDA: Did you finish the book? I can give you another one.

ANTHONY: Not quite.

MIRANDA: How far did you get?

ANTHONY: Twenty pages or so. About.

MIRANDA: *(Suspicious)* What's your favorite poem?

ANTHONY: The first one?

MIRANDA: You haven't read any of it.

ANTHONY: I had to watch the game.

MIRANDA: For a month?

ANTHONY: I have E S P N. I read the jacket. Poems are hard for me. I'd rather look at your beautiful face.

MIRANDA: My face is not beautiful.

ANTHONY: Well, from some angles. Do you like the pen pin?

MIRANDA: *(Admiring)* It's a quill.

ANTHONY: I wanted gold, but they didn't have it.

MIRANDA: I don't deserve a present.

ANTHONY: "Deserve" is not why you give a present.

MIRANDA: You give a present so you get more sex.

ANTHONY: Yeah—no! You give a present because you're passing the store and you see something and it makes you want to give it to your beloved. It's a way of saying that a beautiful person is constantly in my thoughts.

MIRANDA: *(Thinking of* CARL*)* It makes me feel guilty.

ANTHONY: You have nothing to feel guilty about.

MIRANDA: How can somebody be that happy with no memory?

ANTHONY: Faking.

MIRANDA: Let's have sex.

ANTHONY: Not while you're thinking about your happy husband.

MIRANDA: Sex stops me from thinking.

ANTHONY: She's right on the other side of the wall so you can't squeal.

MIRANDA: I don't squeal.

Scene Three

(Later. CARL *the house, books, magazines, a photo album, a bucket by the door.* MIRANDA *enters with her school papers.)*

CARL: Hi, hi.

MIRANDA: What's the bucket doing here?

CARL: It was full. I dumped it on the tree.

MIRANDA: That's what *I* do. So we don't waste water.

CARL: I don't do that?

MIRANDA: You call the plumber. I'll put this back before we have a flood.

CARL: I fixed it. The drip.

MIRANDA: *(Excited)* You remembered how?

CARL: I looked online. I changed the round thing.

MIRANDA: Oh. I guess I could have done that. What do you have there?

CARL: Books, articles, magazines, photo album.

MIRANDA: Is anything familiar?

CARL: My writing is familiar, but…incomplete. I remember *exactly the words I wrote,* but none of the extras—the weather, the sounds. The only real memories are since I woke up. *(Photo album)* The photos of me are "familiar".

MIRANDA: That's from before we met. Your life before.

CARL: I'm really young. *(Holds up a book)* I read the archeologist's biography.

MIRANDA: It was very popular.

CARL: I don't know why— *(Quoting)* "Begin with laudatory praise, go on and on endlessly, then identify a small flaw and inflate it to *monstrous proportions* until subject is thoroughly diminished." *(He smiles)* What?

MIRANDA: You're quoting the one bad review.

CARL: *(Happy)* I saw it online.

MIRANDA: There were good reviews, too.

CARL: I agree with the bad one. Wasn't the archeologist mad?

MIRANDA: He stopped taking your calls.

CARL: Yes, I wouldn't talk to me either. What are all those papers?

MIRANDA: Poems. I have to grade them.

CARL: "A through F."

MIRANDA: These guys don't get an F. If they write anything at all, it passes. When they don't do the assignment, that's an F.

CARL: Nothing equals F?

MIRANDA: In *my* class.

CARL: What gets an A?

MIRANDA: Almost nothing gets an A.

CARL: *(Amused by the concepts)* "*Nothing*" gets an F. "*Almost* nothing" gets an A.

MIRANDA: *(Amused)* I look for a strong metaphor, lyrical language, imagery. I want them to be great, but…well, it's hard to write a great poem.

CARL: Because of the rhymes.

MIRANDA: No. Because of the emotion, the life, the history, the entire reality that has to be evoked.

CARL: "Evoked."

MIRANDA: A lot of poets like rhymes—the sound, the alliteration. But you can look so hard for a rhyme you end up changing the meaning of the poem. I don't write like that.

CARL: You evoke emotion.

MIRANDA: *(Joking)* Well. Sometimes I just rhyme.

CARL: "How now brown clow *duh*."

MIRANDA: Where did that come from?

CARL: It came to me while I was looking at the brown cloud. Did you see it?

MIRANDA: When I went out...for lunch.

CARL: Is it right— Clou-*duh*?

MIRANDA: "How now brown *cow*."

CARL: Cow. Bovine. Milk. Cud. Four stomachs.

MIRANDA: All those things.

CARL: I watched the brown cloud move across the sky.

MIRANDA: You shouldn't sit outside. It's too hot.

CARL: Yes. I got "parched."

MIRANDA: You can get a burn even through a cloud. And you can hurt your eyes.

CARL: *(Triumphant)* I wore the glasses!

MIRANDA: The glasses—? They're for an eclipse.

CARL: I know! I knew immediately when I saw them in the drawer. I went outside to look for an eclipse and saw the cloud instead.

MIRANDA: Did you also know you're not supposed to look at the sun for more than fifteen minutes, even with the glasses?

CARL: Oh. No.

MIRANDA: I told you to call me if you had questions.

CARL: But I didn't have a question- I had an answer. I didn't know it was incomplete.

MIRANDA: How long did you sit out there?

CARL: Not long. It's so hot.

MIRANDA: I know. Water the tree and the water evaporates before it hits the ground. The investigators think that was why the utility pole fell—the subcontractors didn't use enough water when they mixed the cement.

CARL: What is negative rainfall? I looked online. We get negative rainfall.

MIRANDA: The water we pipe in evaporates. It's called negative rainfall.

CARL: It comes from the ground?

MIRANDA: Deeper and deeper. And we steal it from the Colorado. You said not to worry about it.

CARL: I said that?

MIRANDA: When I got the job. I said people shouldn't live in a desert.
You said it is man's obligation to use the world's resources.

CARL: Judiciously?! Did I say use them *judiciously*? Did I say "share"?

MIRANDA: I never heard you say "share".

CARL: But I love *share*. I saw the word and I knew what it meant, and it made me feel—it made me want to do it. Share. Say it.

MIRANDA: …Share.

CARL: Doesn't that make you want to do it?

(MIRANDA *needs to change the subject.*)

MIRANDA: …Did you recognize anybody else in the photographs?

CARL: No. I assume the two old people are my dead parents.

MIRANDA: Yes.

CARL: What are all these vehicles?

MIRANDA: Farm equipment.

CARL: I was a farmer?

MIRANDA: You were never a farmer. You wouldn't even help your Dad. When you were in high school you got a job at the drug store, so you could help them financially, but you wouldn't help on the farm.

CARL: Was I a...um. Won't-kill-animals?

MIRANDA: It wasn't that kind of farm.

CARL: What's the word for that? Won't-kill-animals.

MIRANDA: I don't think there is one.

CARL: There should be.

MIRANDA: You just didn't like farming. You left Minnesota when you went to college. You got a Bachelor of Science degree from the University of Virginia. You went to graduate school, but you left when you started making money writing science articles. You thought school was boring and too slow. You learned more on your own. Reading what was relevant. Skipping the inessential.

CARL: "Inessential."

MIRANDA: Like poetry.

CARL: *(Horrified)* I said poetry was inessential?

MIRANDA: Not right away.

CARL: I can't believe I said that to you.

MIRANDA: Right out loud.

CARL: That was mean. *(Horrified)* Was I mean to you?

MIRANDA: *(Changing the subject)* Do you want me to put that away?

CARL: No, I... No. I saw our wedding pictures. My mother is in them.

MIRANDA: Your Dad was too sick to come. We spent our honeymoon at his hospital.

CARL: I'm sorry.

MIRANDA: Please...don't say that.

CARL: But I'm sorry.

MIRANDA: We should keep it clinical.

CARL: Did the doctor say to keep it clinical?

MIRANDA: *(Some edge)* It's the only way—Carl. ...You are washed clean of me. It's like I never happened to you. I have to keep it clinical. Do you understand that?

CARL: I don't.

MIRANDA: It's like I'm erased.

CARL: I'm trying to put you back.

MIRANDA: Okay, I know.

(Brief pause. CARL *thinks this might be safe.)*

CARL: How did we meet?

MIRANDA: I was giving a reading at a bookstore in Pittsburgh. It wasn't a real book tour. I was hopping around the Midwest going to cities where I had friends with sleep sofas. You came in to buy a book on insects. I thought you'd come for the poetry.

CARL: I lied?

MIRANDA: You let me believe it for a long time. A few years later, we were having a fight. It came out.

CARL: What happened after Pittsburgh?

MIRANDA: I thought it was over. A great fling that ended too fast because we were geographically incorrect. A few weeks later you showed up in Brooklyn with your laptop and a toothbrush. You wrote science for a lot of money at the table and I wrote poems nobody wanted on the bed.

CARL: I like your poems.

MIRANDA: You remember them?

CARL: The books.

MIRANDA: *(Horrified, accusingly)* Did you go in my office?!

CARL: No, I...I have them in *my* office. Am I not allowed to go in your office?

MIRANDA: No, you can...there's just...there's things I haven't told you. I keep a journal. You do, too. We always have. *(An order)* We don't read each other's.

CARL: Okay—

MIRANDA: It's really important.

CARL: I see that.

MIRANDA: I didn't read yours—even when- even when you were in the coma. I thought...

CARL: What did you think?

MIRANDA: I thought if I read them you would die...and we had vowed.

CARL: "Vow."

MIRANDA: Could you...could you not do that? That repeating the word thing. It's like you're savoring them.

CARL: "Savor" —no, I'm sorry. I'm sorry. I'm trying.

MIRANDA: It's just...it's too different. You're too different.

CARL: What was I?

MIRANDA: We shouldn't do this. *(An excuse)* It might not be good for you.

CARL: We have to do it some time. I have to know. Don't you think I have to know?

MIRANDA: You might freak out.

CARL: I promise I won't freak out.

MIRANDA: It's just… *(Then firmly)* you had stopped talking.

CARL: *(Laughs)* What? Why would I do that?

MIRANDA: You were sick of words.

CARL: Not possible. Snowflake? Onomatopoeia? Evoke!

MIRANDA: You said they were used to harm.

CARL: "To harm." …Like when I "diminished" the archeologist?

MIRANDA: Yes. You said you were sick of the harm they caused. You couldn't even bear to talk. I asked you, why are you so silent, are you mad at me? You said you weren't, you were sick of words, you decided not to say anything you'd ever said before. You were going to…to wow me with an entirely new assemblage of words.

CARL: "Assem"— *(Shuts his mouth quickly)* Did I? Did I wow you?

MIRANDA: You did not.

CARL: *(Hopeful)* I must have been collecting the words. I was happily being quiet as the new "assemblage" took place.

MIRANDA: *(Some edge)* You weren't happily anything. It was a long time.

CARL: Always? Was I always not happily?

MIRANDA: No. There were great years.

CARL: I'm happy now.

MIRANDA: Even when you were happy, you weren't like this.

CARL: Is it bad? That I'm like this?

MIRANDA: It is... *(Realizing, greatly surprised)* not bad. That you are like this.

CARL: Tell me the *vow*. The don't-read-the-journals one.

MIRANDA: *(Can't go there)* I don't remember—we just promised.

CARL: I *vow*, I *re*-vow, that I will not read your journal.

MIRANDA: Thank you. *(A safe topic)* I didn't know you kept copies of my books.

CARL: I have two. Are there more?

MIRANDA: There's four.

CARL: My two are very sexy.

MIRANDA: They're the ones that sell.

CARL: I've almost worn them out.

MIRANDA: You can't have—

CARL: Yes, they seem very worn out. The... spines are busted.

MIRANDA: Really?

CARL: Yes, I hope you'll give me new ones.

MIRANDA: Yes, I will.

CARL: One of the articles I wrote, "Female sexuality". I borrowed phrases from your poems.

MIRANDA: Stole. Also for the book you co-authored.

CARL: There's a whole book on female sexuality?

MIRANDA: One you co-authored. We have no copy. Somebody is always borrowing it and keeping it.

CARL: It's hot?

MIRANDA: A sizzler.

CARL: Orgasms.

MIRANDA: Everybody's favorite topic.

CARL: Vaginal and clitoral.

MIRANDA: Well, the debate rolls on.

CARL: Like the orgasm. The "rolling orgasm" in the poem. *Rolling.*

MIRANDA: *(Amused in spite of herself)* I know.

CARL: "Necks outstretched, bodies entwined, a cry reaching for the moon." Did you write that about us?

MIRANDA: It's from before we met.

CARL: Oh… Who did you write it about?

MIRANDA: A pair of Laysan albatrosses. But nobody would buy the book if they knew it was about gooney birds.

CARL: What makes them so sexy?

MIRANDA: They mate for life.

(Brief pause)

CARL: Thank you for allowing me to steal some poetry phrases.

MIRANDA: Well. More people read them in your books than mine.

CARL: Would you read poems to me? I'd like to hear them out loud.

MIRANDA: I have to…I told you, I don't recite my poems. I have to go to bed. *(A brief glance at him)* Don't stay up too late.

(MIRANDA exits. CARL watches her.)

Scene 4

(Thursday, late morning. A Coffeeshop. CARL *with books at a table.* ANTHONY *enters, surprised to see* CARL. ANTHONY *looks to see if* MIRANDA *is there—nope. He lurks, approaches.)*

ANTHONY: Hey, Mister? Is that you on the back of that book?

CARL: Oh, yes. Yes, it's me. I wrote it.

ANTHONY: Is it any good?

CARL: *(Triumph)* It monstrously inflates a small flaw.

ANTHONY: Should that make you so happy?

CARL: I don't know.

ANTHONY: *(Looking at the book)* I know you. You write for *Science Today.*

CARL: I do?

ANTHONY: Can I buy you a round?

CARL: A round what?

ANTHONY: Another one of those.

CARL: *(Discovers)* The rim of the cup! Round!

ANTHONY: I'll get you a fresh one.

CARL: No thanks. Caffeine really works. *(Brief pause)* Oh! I know what happens now. *(Stands, then formally)* Would you like to join me?

ANTHONY: Thank you, I'd love to.

*(*ANTHONY *sits,* CARL *doesn't.)*

ANTHONY: You can sit, too.

CARL: Thank you. I'm Carl.

ANTHONY: *(Referencing the book)* I see that.

CARL: *(Proud of his consideration)* And you are?

ANTHONY: Anthony. *(The book)* Nice photo.

CARL: I was younger.

ANTHONY: Yeah.

CARL: And my hair was longer. It's growing back now.

ANTHONY: I thought maybe you were military.

CARL: I'm not that. Or maybe I am. I'll ask.

ANTHONY: *(Re: the book jacket)* This is about a dig.

CARL: Archeology.

ANTHONY: *(Reading the back of the book; his probe starts here.)* Wow. You spent ten months with this guy.

CARL: *(Correcting)* Ten months *off and on*. In China.

ANTHONY: That's a long time to be away from home.

CARL: It was *off and on*.

ANTHONY: Still. The family and all.

CARL: Oh yes. My Wife.

ANTHONY: She must have missed you. *(Urgently)* Did she miss you?

CARL: She didn't say. Or she might have said, and I don't remember.

ANTHONY: Yes, a wife can get very lonely in ten months.

CARL: *(Correcting)* Ten months *off and on*.

ANTHONY: But then you get to have the joyous, *joyous* reunion. Very sexy. You and your wife. A lot of... joyousness.

CARL: I wish I could remember—the accident.

ANTHONY: Something happened to your wife?

CARL: No, she wasn't there. A utility pole fell on my car.

ANTHONY: That sounds wrong.

CARL: I know. But there are many witnesses. Proof that whatever happened, someone-who-isn't-me is responsible: the *police* who neglected to report the earlier accident that weakened the integrity of the pole; the *subtractor*, who might have used insufficient water in the cement; *God*, who might have produced one of His "acts of"; anybody but the electric company who is responsible for nothing except collecting our money.

ANTHONY: What's a subtractor?

CARL: I don't know. *(Guessing)* A minus-er?

ANTHONY: You said a subtractor might have used insufficient cement.

CARL: I must have meant something else. What could I have meant?

ANTHONY: Sub*con*tractor?

CARL: Yes. Subcontractor— Sub. The sub people do everything. Layers of possible blame so that nothing reaches the top. But he, or she, cannot hide- someone will pay. The lawyer promises I will clean up because much of me has been- subtracted! By the Subtractor. Whoever it turns out to be.

ANTHONY: You were in the hospital?

CARL: Two months.

ANTHONY: And then you came home.

CARL: Yes.

ANTHONY: Did you have a joyous reunion? When you got home from the hospital? *(No reply)* It must have been joyous. Your reunion. After two months. Very joyous. With your wife.

CARL: Not so much joyous-ness. One of the subtractions. I suppose.

ANTHONY: *(Great relief)* Well. I'm very sorry about your subtraction. Two months is a lot of time to lose.

CARL: One month in a coma. One month for observation and to read the dictionary.

ANTHONY: Why would you want to read the dictionary?

CARL: To look up words that don't self-identify.

ANTHONY: Which ones self-identify?

CARL: *(Greatly amused at* ANTHONY*)* Oh my goodness. Chair?

ANTHONY: What about it?

CARL: *(Everyone knows this)* Self-identifies. When you see the word chair, it asserts itself, you know what it is even if you don't know what it is. You see those five little letters and then the brain provides you with the picture: wooden appliance, four legs, a back, a seat. From just five letters. That's a miracle.

ANTHONY: *(Annoyed)* That's not what I see.

CARL: *(Astonished)* You don't see a chair?

ANTHONY: Not a wooden one. Mine is big and soft. A recliner.

CARL: Why would you see a *recliner* when we're talking about a *chair*?

ANTHONY: They're synonyms. *(Annoyed)* And there's no miracle.

CARL: Yes, I think so.

ANTHONY: No. You have the order wrong. It's object first then the word. You *see* a chair when you see *the word* chair because you already know what a chair is. There is no miracle!

(Brief pause, CARL *is wide-eyed, holding his breath.)*

CARL: *(Triumph)* Awkward!

ANTHONY: What?!

CARL: Yes. I was wondering how to describe what I was feeling, and it came to me. "Awkward."

ANTHONY: Yes.

CARL: It came to me like a miracle.

(Brief pause, then ANTHONY changes the subject.)

ANTHONY: Is there pain? From the subtraction?

CARL: Oh, no. I feel no pain. I feel…enormous. Is that right?

ANTHONY: I don't think so.

CARL: Wait, I'll show you. *(He gets the astronaut book from his bag)* I wrote this one, too—as a ghost, see, no photo of me—but that's not the point. The point is this: the book takes place in space. I didn't go to space, but I remember it. Vividly. That means—

ANTHONY: I know what it means.

CARL: Listen to this. *(Reads)* "The sky looks quiet when you're on earth, but space is never quiet. The noises from the life-sustaining apparatuses pound in our heads all day and all night. There is never a silence. They give us earplugs for sleeping, but the earplug quiet is filled with the sound of my own heart, and the hearing of the heart turns sleep into a ponderous meditation on mortality. *(Slow heartbeats)* Lub *dub*, lub *dub*, I *live*, for *now*, I *live*, for *now*."

ANTHONY: Vivid.

CARL: Yes, but let me ask you, just now, when I was reading, did it make you *remember*?

ANTHONY: I don't understand.

CARL: Did what I was reading feel like your memory?

ANTHONY: No. It's vivid, but it's not a memory.

CARL: Yes, for you it's merely vivid. For me I was *there* in the vast sky with the noise and the sound of my heart. For me, it's part of my life. And *that* makes me feel *enormous*.

ANTHONY: ...It's like we're on an airplane.

CARL: I don't remember.

ANTHONY: It's how people talk on an airplane—to a stranger. Somebody they'll never see again.

CARL: We are not strangers. We are Carl and Anthony. I know your name because I asked. I was not self-involved. Not like before. She says I'm very different.

ANTHONY: She? Your wife?

CARL: I was silent, a silence that consumes everything around it—a black hole of silence. Doesn't that sound bad?

ANTHONY: *(Seizes the moment)* Bad? No...no, it doesn't sound bad at all. *(Starts to create his scheme, making it up as he goes along)* Listen...if that's how you are, a black hole, whatever, then that's how you should be. You should embrace your soul-sucking personality and let it reign.

CARL: I don't want to be like that.

ANTHONY: But if you *are* like that, you should be allowed to *be* like that.

CARL: But I'm not like that. I'm happy.

ANTHONY: You mustn't be happy.

CARL: Yes, I must be.

ANTHONY: No. If you're happy *(Thinks this up right now)* she won't do anything to *make you happy*. You want her to make you happy, don't you?

CARL: Who is she?

ANTHONY: Your wife. *(Pretending an epiphany)* I'll bet that's why she married you. She likes silent, light-sucking husbands. So she has to work really hard to make you happy.

(Brief pause)

CARL: Do you have a wife?

ANTHONY: Divorced.

(CARL chokes, gags.)

ANTHONY: What?

CARL: *(Looks in his dictionary!)* What is that word?

ANTHONY: Divorced?

CARL: Ouch.

ANTHONY: It means you're not married any more.

CARL: I've never heard it.

ANTHONY: Oh, you've heard it.

CARL: It sounds like a snake. A hissing dangerous snake attack. "Divorsss-*tuh*." It's a terrible word.

ANTHONY: A word you want to avoid at all costs?

CARL: Oh, yes.

ANTHONY: I can help you here. Since my divorce—

CARL: Ouch, ow—

ANTHONY: Okay, that has to stop. Say it. Say the word.

CARL: No.

ANTHONY: Say it so it has no power over you. You say it, you own it, you are unafraid. Deee—

CARL: Deee—

ANTHONY: Vorce.

CARL: Vorce. Ow.

ANTHONY: No, you're fine. Since my *divorce*! I've done a lot of research.

CARL: Books?

ANTHONY: Oh, yes. Books, articles, magazines. There's a lot written about this, but I will crystallize it for you, so you don't have to read any books. If you want a woman to be yours forever, you must be morose. You must be...*indifferent* to her. Once you are indifferent, she gets obsessed with trying to make you happy.

CARL: I'd like that.

ANTHONY: If you want your wife to be interested, you must keep her intrigued! By making her think you are indifferent; indifferent to food, indifferent to art, indifferent to sex, *particularly*. She won't be able to get enough of you. Indifference is the essence of human desire.

CARL: "Essence."

ANTHONY: *(Correcting)* Indifference. You don't talk to her. You stay in your office.

CARL: *(Amazed)* How could you tell I have an office?

ANTHONY: *(Caught)* ...You're a writer, I assumed the office. Do you? Have one.

CARL: I do.

ANTHONY: Right. Stay in there. You are indifferent. *(Idea)* And the other thing you must cultivate along with indifference is your *masculine audacity*.

CARL: Oh! I don't know what that is. Is it in the dictionary?

ANTHONY: Masculine audacity. You are a manly man *growling* your displeasures.

CARL: Growling?

ANTHONY: She won't be able to get enough of it. You want that, don't you?

CARL: Yes, yes. I want it. …I want it.

(ANTHONY *growls*. CARL *growls*.)

Scene Five

(Later, night, the house. CARL *reads a book; there is a big box labeled "Carl's journals."* MIRANDA *enters.)*

MIRANDA: Hi.

CARL: *(Amazed, holding up book)* Punctuated equilibrium.

MIRANDA: What's that?

CARL: *(Reads)* "Punctuated equilibrium is a series of sudden abrupt changes in a species, rather than the popular notion of long, slow, gradual evolution." I relate to the abrupt-change theory having recently had an abrupt change myself.

MIRANDA: Who's the writer?

CARL: Stephen Jay Gould, Paleontologist.

MIRANDA: You have a lot of his books.

CARL: Six.

MIRANDA: You've always been very enthusiastic about him.

CARL: *(Oops)* Enthusiastic?

MIRANDA: You quote him a lot.

CARL: *(Struggling to get on task)* I don't feel so… enthusiastic.

MIRANDA: He won't let science be used to hurt people. You like that.

CARL: I'm more...indifferent. I'm— I'm...indifferent to him.

MIRANDA: You like him. What's for dinner?

CARL: Dinner?

MIRANDA: You're making us dinner.

CARL: I ate the leftovers.

MIRANDA: You said you were cooking for us. You said so at breakfast.

CARL: I must have changed my mind. Or forgot. I must have forgot. To remember.

MIRANDA: I'll get a sandwich. Do you want anything?

CARL: I am indifferent to food.

MIRANDA: *(What is going on here?)* You're...? Since when?

CARL: Since...recently.

MIRANDA: You weren't indifferent to food at breakfast—six waffles.

CARL: More recently than breakfast.

MIRANDA: Apparently, you weren't indifferent when you ate the leftovers.

CARL: They were very good.

MIRANDA: You aren't "indifferent to food", Carl. You're just not hungry. There's a difference.

CARL: What's the difference?

MIRANDA: Not hungry is temporary. Indifferent to food is permanent. You're "not hungry" because you ate the very delicious leftovers.

CARL: I'm feeling indifferent to food.

MIRANDA: *(Growing annoyance)* You're feeling indifferent to Stephen Jay Gould—you're feeling indifferent to food. Let's see… *(Looking around, refers to the box)* Are you feeling indifferent to your journals?

CARL: Fully. I'm going to put the box back in the closet.

MIRANDA: *(An edge)* Read them. You might remember something.

CARL: I also might not.

MIRANDA: Well it couldn't get much worse!

CARL: *(A fact)* It would be worse.

MIRANDA: Fine.

(MIRANDA starts for the kitchen. To stop her, CARL growls, puffs up, stands tall.)

MIRANDA: What are you doing?! Stop that.

CARL: It's how I'm feeling. Like growling. Standing tall and growling. Like a man. *(Growls)*

MIRANDA: You sound like a Rottweiler.

CARL: I don't know what that is.

MIRANDA: Read your journals, Carl. Maybe you'll remember something about a Rottweiler. *(Turns to exit.)*

CARL: Please don't—

MIRANDA: Please don't what? Please don't go scrounge up a peanut butter and jelly sandwich after a long hard day?

CARL: *(Fully backtracking)* I remember a movie.

MIRANDA: Swell.

CARL: I saw Nichole Kidman on T V. She was talking to a woman. A hostess.

MIRANDA: A talk show.

CARL: Yes, there was a lot of talking. And I remember seeing her in a movie. It was sexy.

MIRANDA: *(Has had enough of whatever this is)* Okay. Whatever. I'm going to get my sandwich. The one you forgot to remember to make. On purpose!

CARL: It wasn't…

MIRANDA: What?!

CARL: It wasn't "on purpose." I was indifferent.

MIRANDA: Indifferent *is* on purpose!

CARL: I wasn't…I wasn't going to make a sandwich. I was going to make a recipe from a book.

MIRANDA: But for some reason you changed your mind. Your indifferent mind.

CARL: I could make it now.

MIRANDA: No thank you.

CARL: Are you indifferent to my recipe?

MIRANDA: I'm feeling a little indifferent. And a lot hungry. I'm going to make a sandwich and take it to my room. Goodnight, Carl.

(MIRANDA exits. Once she's gone, CARL growls quietly to himself to test a growl; shakes off the growl, then says:)

CARL: *(To himself, nods)* Punctuated equilibrium.

END OF ACT ONE

(Intermission. Ten minutes or so)

ACT TWO

Scene One

(*Friday evening, the dental office.* ANTHONY *and* MIRANDA, *who fiddles with a dental tool with a clown face on the handle. He is putting his clothes back on. She is already redressed.*)

MIRANDA: Fridays always suck. Their brains are on speed and their eyes are on their cell phones. All my attempts at meter and emotion are met with hostility and blank stares.

ANTHONY: Yeah, I always cut class on Friday.

MIRANDA: How did you get through dental school?

ANTHONY: I had the inessential shit on Fridays.

MIRANDA: What, like poetry?

ANTHONY: I never had to take poetry—I mean—I don't know what I mean.

MIRANDA: What is this?

ANTHONY: It's a scraper.

MIRANDA: What do you do with it?

ANTHONY: Scrape teeth.

MIRANDA: Not the kids' teeth.

ANTHONY: Of course. The clown face is so they're not scared of me.

MIRANDA: This face is the stuff of nightmares.

ANTHONY: *(Surprised)* Oh yeah, they cry.

MIRANDA: That should be a clue.

ANTHONY: *(Disappointed)* But I had it made special.

MIRANDA: Get rid of it. They need to see you in some activity. They walk in and they see this big friendly man, dressed as…big bird—

ANTHONY: No.

MIRANDA: You sing Old MacDonald so they can sing along, and then you introduce them to your dental tool—one without a face on the end. You use one of those tooth models—

ANTHONY: Impressions.

MIRANDA: Impressions, yes. You show them how to scrape teeth, let them do it for a minute, and then you say, "now that didn't hurt, did it", and then they happily hop up and open wide.

ANTHONY: That won't work.

MIRANDA: It works when I do it. The first day of class, I get them to suggest some parameters and then before their very eyes I write a bad poem that even the nitwits could write. Calms everybody down.

ANTHONY: …Thanks for coming.

MIRANDA: I told you I'd be here.

ANTHONY: You didn't say you'd be this late. I almost left.

MIRANDA: Why didn't you?

ANTHONY: And go home to what?

MIRANDA: Don't do that—

ANTHONY: No, you're right, I'm sorry. I'm really glad you showed up. How is Carl?

MIRANDA: Don't do that either.

ANTHONY: What? We can't talk about Carl all of a sudden?

MIRANDA: I don't know—it feels like—I don't know.

ANTHONY: What? A betrayal? You think it's a betrayal if we speak about your shit-eating husband?

MIRANDA: He's growling now. Last night, a lot of growls.

(A joy ANTHONY *immediately suppresses.)*

ANTHONY: That's very disturbing.

MIRANDA: No, it's just weird.

ANTHONY: I read up on Carl's illness.

MIRANDA: Where? Nobody's ever seen it before.

ANTHONY: What's his name? The guy who writes about his wife's hat?

MIRANDA: Malcolm Gladwell?

ANTHONY: No, the other guy. He says you have to be really careful.

MIRANDA: I know that, I told you that.

ANTHONY: Not about hurting his feelings. He could be dangerous.

MIRANDA: Carl can't be dangerous.

ANTHONY: This isn't Carl. You said so. He's so changed, you said. There's no telling what he could do. He could do something in his sleep.

MIRANDA: Like walk in his sleep?

ANTHONY: Yes, and rip a door from its hinges. Throw it right at you. While growling.

MIRANDA: He's not a door ripper.

ANTHONY: Yes, but in sleep, he might be enormous—
(The word surprising him) "enormous"…

MIRANDA: What?

ANTHONY: No, I mean—he might have enormous
power. You're not sleeping in the same room, are you?

MIRANDA: Are you making this up to find out if I'm
sleeping with him?

ANTHONY: Hey, I'm the guy worried about your safety.
Look online. Google "sleeping violence".

MIRANDA: It's prejudicial if you include violence in the
search title.

ANTHONY: No, I searched on "head injury", "sleeping
violence" came up on the first page. I just want you
to beware. Be on the lookout for anything out of the
ordinary.

MIRANDA: Everything is out of the ordinary.

ANTHONY: …That looks nice. *(The pin)*

MIRANDA: It stuck me when you were pulling off my
shirt.

ANTHONY: Yeah, it's a trick so you don't forget me.

MIRANDA: I can't forget you—I have a scratch on my
chest.

ANTHONY: Don't let your husband see it.

MIRANDA: My husband won't see it…and even if he
did, he is indifferent.

ANTHONY: *(Happy at that)* You should move out.

MIRANDA: And I will when he can function. He can't
even leave the house.

ANTHONY: *(Doesn't correct her)* Well…if he can't leave
the house, that's good! Then he can't accidentally see

you walking into my condo building. You can come over.

MIRANDA: Your wife comes there.

ANTHONY: Ex wife. To get her check and then she's gone. You should come over. See my bed. My brand-new bed, king-size.

MIRANDA: King-size sheets are very expensive.

ANTHONY: Particularly the silk ones.

MIRANDA: *(Impressed)* You got silk sheets?

ANTHONY: Staying in their box until you come over. But in the meantime…

(ANTHONY *reaches into his pocket, hands* MIRANDA *an envelope.)*

MIRANDA: What did you do—? No more presents.

ANTHONY: No, you'll like it. Ladies like it.

MIRANDA: *(Reads)* A spa visit?

ANTHONY: A whole day. Or you can go twice, a half day each time. Go tomorrow. They pamper you. Massage, facial, steam bath, haircut, highlights, you can get highlights.

MIRANDA: Who are you trying to make me look like?

ANTHONY: Nobody! It's fun. It's for ladies. They're in and out of there all day long. It's next to my building. You can come over after and show me what they did.

MIRANDA: Will I run into Angie?

ANTHONY: You will just run into me. Do you like it?

MIRANDA: It's nice.

ANTHONY: Is it nice enough for a special thank you?

MIRANDA: Thank you.

ANTHONY: No, you know. Special. In the chair. *(The word surprising him)* Chair...

MIRANDA: ...What?

ANTHONY: What do you see when I say chair?

MIRANDA: Well, right now, I see a very high dental chair.

ANTHONY: Yeah, me too.

MIRANDA: *(Saying no to "special thank you".)* A chair I *just had* sex in—I have to get home.

ANTHONY: Maybe you have to work late.

MIRANDA: He'll worry.

ANTHONY: Maybe we don't care.

MIRANDA: I have to make sure he eats.

ANTHONY: He's indifferent to food. *(Quickly)* You said so. Didn't you? It's already late, so stay. Stay until he's asleep. I really need you to. You don't owe him an explanation, you don't owe him anything. Don't go. Please don't go.

(It is clear MIRANDA is not going any place any time soon.)

Scene Two

(Saturday early afternoon, the house. CARL is there, perhaps just waking up, buttoning his clothing, he looks toward the kitchen, grows increasingly agitated as he realizes MIRANDA is not there. He looks out the window, he looks at his watch, he hyperventilates, he puts his head between his knees, he cries out a whimper. He holds his breath as the door opens and she enters, she is re-done, head-to-toe, dressed how we might imagine ANTHONY's ex to dress.)

CARL: Where were you—?! Are you alright? You didn't come home last night. I didn't know what to do.

MIRANDA: I came home. You were asleep. I went to bed.

CARL: You weren't here this morning.

MIRANDA: I was. You were asleep when I left.

CARL: The grinder wakes me.

MIRANDA: I got coffee out.

CARL: It's Saturday. You don't have work.

MIRANDA: I had an appointment.

CARL: All morning?

MIRANDA: Yes, it took a long time.

CARL: You didn't leave a note.

MIRANDA: I didn't think it was necessary. You're indifferent.

(Brief pause as CARL examines MIRANDA.)

CARL: You look different.

MIRANDA: Yes. It was quite extensive.

CARL: What? What was extensive?

MIRANDA: *(Disdainfully)* I had a Spa morning.

CARL: What's that?

MIRANDA: A place to be pampered and redone. I am fully spa'd.

CARL: You're glowing. What did they do to you?

MIRANDA: I arrived. They sent me into a changing room. Leave everything behind. Everything. Including underwear.

CARL: Like the hospital.

MIRANDA: Yes. Except for the fluffy robe instead of the paper thing with the open rear end. Then the steam room to open my pores. Then the cold shower to close them.

CARL: What are pores?

MIRANDA: Things that need opening and closing. Then the mask.

CARL: Tribal? Carnival? Bandit?

MIRANDA: A cream for the face to make my skin soft.

CARL: Can I touch it?

MIRANDA: It isn't soft any more.

CARL: How come?

MIRANDA: Because now it's covered with makeup.

CARL: You wear makeup?

MIRANDA: I do today. And toenail polish.

CARL: *(Looking at her open-toed shoes)* They're really red.

MIRANDA: A pedicurist used a vegetable peeler to remove my foot calluses.

CARL: Ouch.

MIRANDA: She collected a huge pile of dead foot skin in a towel on the floor. I almost heaved my breakfast. But then she started rubbing my feet with lotion. It was glorious. It was the only good part.

CARL: I have lotion from the hospital. I could rub them.

(MIRANDA doesn't respond to this offer.)

CARL: Your hair looks nice.

MIRANDA: You like it better this way?

CARL: It looks nice, but not nicer.

MIRANDA: It was included, the cut and color. I thought, why not? Now, I don't even recognize me.

CARL: I recognize you—don't be worried.

MIRANDA: She fussed with a brush and hairdryer for forty minutes. I don't even have a hairdryer.

CARL: Do you need a brush? You can use mine. I don't need it yet. And even if I did need it I'd share it with you— "Share".

MIRANDA: They did my colors. I'm a winter.

CARL: Then we should definitely move.

MIRANDA: *(Looking at her new outfit)* I don't even own anything this shiny.

CARL: You look really different.

MIRANDA: Yes, I don't usually look like a hooker from the Strip.

CARL: You look better than they look.

MIRANDA: How do you know what they look like?

CARL: I saw them on Thursday.

MIRANDA: You're not allowed to drive.

CARL: Bus. Are you going to make a poem about your spa visit?

MIRANDA: Nothing is coming to mind.

CARL: Nothing rhymes with spa?

MIRANDA: Blah, Ta da, Com çi com ça. I hated it. I was bored and I was angry that this exists and that people think it's a good use of money or that any of it is necessary or that it makes people look good.

CARL: I like how you look.

MIRANDA: No, you don't.

CARL: I like it. I am aroused.

MIRANDA: No, you're not. I'm going to change—

CARL: It's not the clothes. I was aroused already. *(He holds up a book.)* Poem Book Number Two. These are not about birds.

MIRANDA: How can you tell?

CARL: It's dedicated to me. Plus birds do not have palms of the hand. Or teeth. *(From memory)* "Your teeth press in the center of my palm, I feel you all the way down, one plus one is one." That was hard for me. Because I know that one plus one is two.

MIRANDA: It isn't math. It's metaphor. You don't sound particularly indifferent this morning.

CARL: I am not indifferent. Can I put my teeth on your palm?

MIRANDA: It's not a good idea.

CARL: It might be a really good idea.

MIRANDA: *(An excuse)* It isn't clinical.

CARL: Like this? *(He puts his teeth into his own palm, his eyes fixed on her.)*

MIRANDA: Don't bite. Pull your teeth slowly across your palm. *(She watches. She gets turned on, small gasp.)*

CARL: It feels good. Try it.

(MIRANDA runs her teeth across her palm. Her breathing changes.)

CARL: Good, yeah? Auto-cannibalism.

MIRANDA: That's not a word.

CARL: But it's a concept.

MIRANDA: I have to go—

CARL: You don't have work.

MIRANDA: Student. Conference.

(MIRANDA exits. CARL runs his teeth across his palm again.)

CARL: *(Quietly to himself)* Please don't go.

Scene Three

(Later. The dentist office. ANTHONY *and* MIRANDA, *both nervous, standing apart. He intermittently puts a hand into a pocket; she will eventually notice.)*

MIRANDA: The parking lot is empty. Don't dentists work on weekends anymore?

ANTHONY: Only the ones still paying off their loans.

(Brief pause. There is awkwardness in the room)

MIRANDA: Do you have some place you need to be? I didn't mean to pull you away. It was sort of an emergency.

ANTHONY: No, no. I don't have anything.

MIRANDA: I really need you.

ANTHONY: Here I am.

MIRANDA: I wanted to show you all this before it falls apart.

ANTHONY: Why is it going to fall apart?

MIRANDA: Because it took fourteen people to put it together. I'm feeling very sexy.

ANTHONY: Well. I love the shoes.

MIRANDA: I'll kill myself on campus.

ANTHONY: I'm sorry.

MIRANDA: I'm not complaining. I'm just…expressing my gratitude in an awkward fashion.

ANTHONY: *(Erupting with a* CARL *word)* "Awkward."

MIRANDA: I didn't know clothes were going to be part of the spa day.

ANTHONY: Oh. Well, I just got you what Ang- Angie always gets. I mean…what the bill says. I got the same one. For you.

MIRANDA: I can't wear this to school.

ANTHONY: All the kids do.

MIRANDA: And I shouldn't look like them. Even if it sort of makes me feel like them.

ANTHONY: Did Carl see you?

MIRANDA: I don't want to talk about Carl.

ANTHONY: *(Scuffling)* No, of course not. ...Did you like it- the spa?

MIRANDA: I did—I'm really grateful.

ANTHONY: It made you feel good?

MIRANDA: I'm thinking you're deserving a special "thank you".

ANTHONY: *(Backing away)* Yeah, you look great.

MIRANDA: So why are you standing way over there—?

ANTHONY: I'm not—

MIRANDA: When your grateful little poet is five feet across the room?

ANTHONY: *(Lying)* It's just. I don't. Have anything.

MIRANDA: What do you need?

ANTHONY: A condom?

MIRANDA: They're in your secret drawer—

(ANTHONY *blocks* MIRANDA's *way.*)

ANTHONY: No, there's nothing there.

MIRANDA: There was something there last night.

ANTHONY: I… took them home.

MIRANDA: What good are they there? We do it here. In the chair.

ANTHONY: *(Another* CARL *word erupts)* Chair!

MIRANDA: What?!

ANTHONY: *(Scuffle)* I was feeling...optimistic. Like you would...come over. ...You would go to the spa and come right to my condo in your made-up-ness. See my great big bed. We would have sex in my great big bed. So I took the condoms home. And there aren't any here. Where we are now. Why didn't you come directly to my condo?! Like I expected.

MIRANDA: I came to your condo. I left because I saw Angie's Beemer in the lot.

ANTHONY: Oh shit.

MIRANDA: And I didn't particularly want to run into her.

ANTHONY: She was barely there. At all.

MIRANDA: I waited ten minutes.

ANTHONY: Oh, God—

MIRANDA: I couldn't stand outside waiting any longer- I'd have melted.

ANTHONY: Well. It would have only been a minute more...or a few...at the most. And I would have had a big condom there. And you could have seen the apartment and my big bed.

MIRANDA: Well. We could risk it.

ANTHONY: Risk what?

MIRANDA: You know.

ANTHONY: *You said* we shouldn't.

MIRANDA: I changed my mind.

ANTHONY: No, it's a good idea. We should be... consistent.

MIRANDA: Come on. We've been tested.

ANTHONY: Well. That was before.

MIRANDA: Before what? Before Carl came home? Carl and I haven't- I told you we are not sleeping together.

ANTHONY: I know but—

MIRANDA: But you don't believe me.

ANTHONY: No, I do. I do believe you.

MIRANDA: Why would you think I'm having sex with Carl? Did you have sex with Angie? Is that why her car was there?

ANTHONY: *(Caught)* Why—? How can you- how can you even think such a thing?

MIRANDA: Because that would be a guilty reason for you to say I'm having sex with Carl.

ANTHONY: Angie and I are divorced. There is simply no guilty reason. Or chance. That divorced people have sex together. It is much more likely that un-divorced people in the same house have sex together.

MIRANDA: I don't even know you. Who are you? What have you *done*?

ANTHONY: No. Nope. I have done nothing. *(Hand goes in pocket.)*

MIRANDA: What's in your pocket?

ANTIIONY: What—no—

MIRANDA: You keep putting your hand in your pocket.

ANTHONY: It's cold—

MIRANDA: Anthony, did you get me another present?

ANTHONY: Nothing—

MIRANDA: *(Approaching him)* You are such a bad liar- let me see it.

ANTHONY: I—

(MIRANDA *puts her hand in his pocket, feels something, pulls it out of his pocket. A ring.* ANTHONY *and* MIRANDA *both look at it.*)

MIRANDA: What— *(Shock)* Oh my. Is this real?

ANTHONY: It's real.

MIRANDA: *(Impressed and appalled)* I didn't know they came this big. It's really big.

ANTHONY: *(In semi-shock)* It's three and a half perfect karats.

MIRANDA: It's big. It's the biggest diamond I've ever seen. Enormous.

ANTHONY: *(Erupting with a* CARL *word)* "Enormous."

MIRANDA: *(Holds it out to him)* But I can't take it.

ANTHONY: *(Gingerly removing it from her hand and quickly putting it in his pocket.)* No worry then. I'll keep it for you. And you'll know it's there. In my pocket. Whenever you want it. Whenever you're ready.

MIRANDA: Just like that? You're not going to try to make me take it?

ANTHONY: I see how set against it you are. I'm no idiot. I have to admire your steadfastness.

MIRANDA: *(Very suspicious)* Let me see it again.

ANTHONY: Why?

MIRANDA: I want to look at it.

ANTHONY: Let's have sex.

MIRANDA: You don't want to risk it.

ANTHONY: No, we can, we should. You want to.

MIRANDA: Let me see the ring.

ANTHONY: I will…let you see the ring after you leave your husband.

MIRANDA: There wouldn't be some inscription to *somebody*? Something written inside that ring, would there be, Anthony?

ANTHONY: *(Not looking at her)* Of course there's something written inside it. Something poetic and beautiful and...

(As MIRANDA *opens the secret drawer. She holds up a string of condoms.)*

MIRANDA: I don't believe it.

ANTHONY: What? Believe what?

MIRANDA: Goodbye, Anthony. *(She looks at her outfit, realizes)* I know who you want me to look like.

*(*MIRANDA *exits.* ANTHONY *looks at the ring.)*

Scene Four

(Later. The coffeehouse. CARL *has a journal.* ANTHONY *enters.)*

ANTHONY: *(Agitated)* You're here. Thank God.

CARL: You're looking for me?

ANTHONY: Yes. I'm looking for you. I have to talk to you about your marriage. I did some more reading—I read books. Last night. I read them. Marriage books. Several.

CARL: *(Re: journal)* I am actively not reading.

ANTHONY: Because...when I gave you that bad advice about indifference and all that, I didn't know your wife. I mean I still don't...know your wife. I didn't know how she might be indifferent...to indifference.

CARL: She wasn't indifferent, she got mad.

ANTHONY: How could I have known that? Yes, you might need another approach. What is your wife like?

CARL: She turns toward the sunlight. Like a flower. A golden flower.

ANTHONY: Yes, it sounds like indifference is not the ticket with your wife.

CARL: I have abandoned indifference.

ANTHONY: *(Sits down, relieved)* Good, it's good you have done that—you should just be yourself.

CARL: I have no idea who that is. Maybe this will tell me. I'm afraid to read it.

ANTHONY: What is it?

CARL: A journal. An old one because I'm too nervous to read a recent one.

ANTHONY: *(Quiet panic)* Your...wife's journal?

CARL: No, I vowed. This is mine. ...What if I read my journal and I still don't remember?

ANTHONY: You can read another one—

CARL: All I remember are movies. They all star Nichole Kidman. She's always a writer, I must go to a lot of movies about writers. She meets a man, I can't quite see him, the actor, the woman I can see, she's Nichole Kidman. She meets the guy in a bookstore and they fall for each other. They go to his nice apartment in some town she doesn't live in, she's on a book tour, but it's on the cheap, she stays with friends, it's Pittsburgh. Three Rivers, a lot of bridges, beautiful scenes of bridges. He adores her, but she leaves, she goes home to Brooklyn, and he doesn't hear from her, and he just decides to pack up and follow her. And it turns out that she adores him, too, and he sets up shop on the fourth floor of her crummy Brooklyn apartment.

ANTHONY: And then what?

CARL: And then he wakes up in the hospital. It's a memory but it's a movie—a movie memory. I don't know how it ends. I really need to know how it ends.

ANTHONY: Maybe you can rent it. What's it called?

CARL: The title is not part of the memory. I know what the guy wants, even though I can't see the actor's face. He wants her. I feel he wants her very badly, but I don't know what she's going to do.

ANTHONY: She's unpredictable.

CARL: Yes. Unpredictable.

ANTHONY: *(Real)* Women always surprise us.

CARL: They do?

ANTHONY: Yeah. Surprise!

(As ANTHONY *plunks the diamond ring on the table.)*

CARL: What's that?

ANTHONY: Angie left it. Unpredictably!

CARL: Do I know her?

ANTHONY: My wife. She came over this morning to show me what she bought with the last month's alimony money.

CARL: A great big diamond?

ANTHONY: No. Victoria's secret.

CARL: She bought a secret?

ANTHONY: Underwear. A bra. Panties. And a garter belt.

CARL: Garter is a snake. Belt is a belt. A belt made out of a snake.

ANTHONY: A snake that lured the viewer into old habits.

CARL: Yes, I'm not following at all.

ANTHONY: My wife came over to show me her new underwear. She was wearing a full-length coat. That should have been a clue. Who wears a coat in Vegas? Except maybe a stripper. Or an ex-wife. She started with the ring, "I can't keep this Anthony. And I can't hock it, because it contains too many great memories— you in the moonlight in the desert, the two of us naked in your car, and you bring out this ring, for which you hocked your entire first year of income from the clinic." By then she's out of her coat and showing me her thong. What was I supposed to do?

CARL: *(Unfamiliar word)* Thong?

ANTHONY: *Thong.* I was hot for my wife. My hot little wife.

CARL: I was hot for mine, too, from her poems.

ANTHONY: Yeah, they're great.

(CARL sees a light shine through a crack. ANTHONY doesn't notice.)

ANTHONY: *(Continues)* There was nothing poetic about this. This was…like the old days. Like the old days. And I fall asleep like the old days. And when I wake up, she's gone, and the ring is on the nightstand, with a note: "I'm ready to take back this ring. I won't always be ready, but I'm ready now. Text me."

CARL: You know my wife's poems?

ANTHONY: No.

CARL: You said, "they're great."

ANTHONY: Well, I wasn't listening when I said it. I don't know what I said. I don't know them.

CARL: They are great.

ANTHONY: I'm not much for poetry. Or reading, even.

CARL: You gave me bad advice—

ANTHONY: Well, I was missing some facts—

CARL: On purpose. *(Suddenly looking up.)* Oh!

ANTHONY: *(Looks up)* What? What are you looking at?

CARL: The words that make everything make sense.

ANTHONY: What are they?

CARL: "Masculine audacity."

ANTHONY: I don't see them.

CARL: Those two and the three others.

ANTHONY: What three others?

CARL: "Punch him now."

Scene Five

(Much later Saturday. The house. MIRANDA has changed her clothes. She dumps the spa ones near the door. She empties CARL's box of journals and reads from one of them. She paces and reads. She is horrified by what she is reading. He enters with his journal and his new black eye.)

MIRANDA: Where have you been? Jesus Christ, where were you?

CARL: Didn't you get my note?

MIRANDA: Your Note?! Your note that says "don't leave me, your adoring husband, Carl"?

CARL: *(Proud)* That's it! It was the first thing I've written since the coma. What do you think?

MIRANDA: I think it's insufficient!

CARL: It's my first try.

MIRANDA: What did you do to your eye?

CARL: A guy punched me.

MIRANDA: Were you in a bar fight?

CARL: I was in a coffee-shop fight.

MIRANDA: What coffee shop?

CARL: By the university.

MIRANDA: That's the one I go to.

CARL: You weren't there.

MIRANDA: I was…elsewhere.

CARL: Are these your spa clothes?

MIRANDA: I'm taking them to Goodwill. I have shed that image.

CARL: Your toes are still red.

MIRANDA: I'll get some remover.

CARL: I like them.

MIRANDA: It's not me. It's somebody else.

CARL: Angie?

MIRANDA: *(Panic)* What?

CARL: They look like somebody named Angie.

MIRANDA: Why did you say that name?

CARL: I said it by mistake.

MIRANDA: Did you read my journal?

CARL: No.

MIRANDA: Who hit you?

CARL: I hit him first.

MIRANDA: I need you to answer my questions!

CARL: Can I answer them later? Can we talk about this instead?

MIRANDA: What is it?

CARL: *My* journal…from last year. I read it.

MIRANDA: Did you remember?

CARL: No. It's just like the other books. An incomplete memory from somebody else's life. But this is my life. The memory should be complete, but that's not the point. The point is I am not this guy, this guy in this journal…I don't know this guy. It feels like a movie. Or fiction. It's incomplete like fiction.

MIRANDA: I'm sorry you lost your past.

CARL: I didn't lose it all. I have words. And movies. And everything since I woke up in the hospital and saw you. Everything since then is real and full and mine. I have a past—it's just really short.

MIRANDA: I broke my vow.

CARL: Your marriage vow? I didn't say that. Forget I said that.

MIRANDA: The vow that said I wouldn't read your journals.

CARL: Are they dark? This one is so dark.

MIRANDA: These are worse.

CARL: How can they be worse? *(Reads)* "I am inundated with the inglorious past while simultaneously overwhelmed by the terrifying future. There is no chance for *now*. No chance to simply *be*, simply *feel*, simply *live*. Now is simply impossible." *(Brief pause)* In your poems you find the light; in my journal I wallow in the dark. How could you stand it?

MIRANDA: I thought you hated me—

CARL: Not possible.

MIRANDA: *(So mad)* You were trying to make me "safe." This house, my job so that I'm "self sufficient." So you could… "leave."

CARL: I don't have any place to go.

MIRANDA: *(Slightly over, referencing the journal)* "I have a job so I don't worry about money. A list of plumbers to call when the drain leaks and electricians when the lights fail. A society of like-minded intellectuals to comfort me when you "leave"!

CARL: Where was I going?

MIRANDA: You were leaving this life!

CARL: There's another life?

MIRANDA: You sad, miserable, *suicidal* idiot—I am so mad at you.

CARL: *(Doesn't know this word)* Sue...is...what? Is that in the dictionary?

MIRANDA: You and your "exit strategy." How dare you?! Never talk to me? Never tell me? Never ask me for help all the while taking *high-paying* jobs that you hate. "One more and there will be enough money for her."

CARL: Who?

MIRANDA: I love you, you shit!

CARL: "Love"?

MIRANDA: *(Furious)* And you love me! And I don't muddle! Where do you get off? Maybe I don't do things like you do them, but I get them done. The bills get paid, the plumber gets called...eventually. I was, and I am, quite self-sufficient.

CARL: Love?

MIRANDA: You idiot.

CARL: Yes, I am. Do the journals say "muddle?"

MIRANDA: They are very critical.

CARL: I inflated small flaws. What was wrong with me?

MIRANDA: *(The whole pain of this word as she hugs a journal)* You were sad. You were so sad.

CARL: I'm not sad now. I mean I'm worried that you're going to leave, and then I'll be sad, but in general, I'm not at all sad.

MIRANDA: Do you have any idea how bad it would be for me if you were to leave?

CARL: I won't leave. Unless you leave, and then I'll go with you.

MIRANDA: I'm not going to leave.

CARL: Then nothing else matters. *(He is smiling. He doesn't know why.)*

MIRANDA: Your eye looks terrible.

CARL: I don't care.

MIRANDA: I like how happy you are.

CARL: Yes, I'm happy. The whole way.

MIRANDA: All you had to do was lose everything.

CARL: I didn't lose "now."

MIRANDA: Here.

CARL: What are those?

MIRANDA: *My journals.*

CARL: I don't need them.

MIRANDA: It's only fair, Carl.

CARL: I don't want fair. I want Miranda.

MIRANDA: You'll know me.

CARL: I know you. I read your poems. ...I vow.

MIRANDA: What?

CARL: I vow I will never read your journals.

MIRANDA: I vow...I don't know what to vow.

CARL: Say a poem. Recite.

(Brief pause)

MIRANDA: "Your teeth press in the center of my palm, I feel you all the way down, one plus one is one."

(MIRANDA exhales deeply then extends her hand; CARL takes it. Salvation. The beginning)

END OF PLAY

www.ingramcontent.com/pod-product-compliance
Lightning Source LLC
Chambersburg PA
CBHW052223090426
42741CB00010B/2654